Learn to Fish

A STEP-BY-STEP GUIDE FOR BEGINNING ANGLERS

Dennis J. Knowles and Gail A. Grizzell

Learn to Fish: A Step-by-Step Guide for Beginning Anglers

www.thefishingfoundation.org

ISBN: 979-8-9858927-1-0 (Paperback)
ISBN: 979-8-9858927-0-3 (Print Replica)

Illustrator Jamie Sale, www.jamiesale-cartoonist.com

Book Designer, Becky's Graphic Design®, LLC
www.beckysgraphicdesign.com

Printed in United States of America

Library of Congress Control Number: 2022904088

Publisher's Cataloging-in-Publication Data

Names: Knowles, Dennis James, author. | Grizzell, Gail Ann, author. | Sale, Jamie, illustrator.

Title: Learn to fish : a step by step guide for beginning anglers / by Dennis James Knowles and Gail Ann Grizzell; [illustrated by Jamie Sale].

Description: Cleveland, OH: Becky Bayne, Becky's Graphic Design, 2022. | Summary: A fishing guide for young people.
Identifiers: LCCN: 2022904088 | ISBN: 979-8-9858927-1-0
Subjects: LCSH Fishing--Juvenile literature. | BISAC JUVENILE NONFICTION / Sports & Recreation / Water Sports | JUVENILE NONFICTION / Sports & Recreation / Camping & Outdoor Activities
Classification: LCC SH439 .K56 2022 | DDC 799.1--dc23

Uncle Ulysses   Miss Margaret

This book is dedicated to outdoor and fishing enthusiasts
Margaret F. Grizzell and Ulysses B. Tidwell.

Margaret Grizzell loved to fish. She frequented the local and regional lakes in northern Ohio and for nearly 40 years made an annual pilgrimage to Martha's Vineyard, Massachusetts, for fishing in the Atlantic Ocean. Margaret instilled a lifelong passion for fishing in her daughter Gail Ann Grizzell, the co-author of this book.

Known as "Uncle U-lis" by his nephew Dennis James Knowles, the co-author of this book, Ulysses B. Tidwell inspired Dennis to take up the sport of fishing after years of fun-filled camping trips along the Mississippi River in Wisconsin.

Preface

THE FISHING FOUNDATION (TFF), a 501(c)3 nonprofit launched in 2012 in Cleveland, Ohio, was created by Dennis James Knowles and Gail Ann Grizzell to encourage youth in the pursuit of a lifelong passion for the sport of fishing. Since 2014, TFF has offered training and classroom instruction on fishing techniques and  regulations, fish habitats, water safety and conservation, and time spent fishing in a safe and secure environment. Program participants enjoy a fun-filled day of learning about casting, rigging, knot-tying, fish species and the importance of sustaining the environment, and fishing from shore.

Through grant support, TFF provides instructional materials, a rod and reel, bait, tackle, and hands-on training by certified fishing instructors—all TFF staff and key volunteers are certified fishing instructors through the Ohio Department of Natural Resources' Passport to Fishing program. In addition, to expand educational impact, we have created this fishing instructional manual for beginner youth anglers to learn how to fish.

It's also important to note that fostering a love for fishing in our youth can only be fully

Dennis James Knowles

accomplished by supporting stewardship of the environment and encouraging our youth to get outdoors. The facts are that today children spend less time in the natural world than past generations. The increased use of computers, cell phones, iPads® and other technologies contributes to a decrease in time spent participating in outdoor activities. Some studies indicate that teens spend less than five hours a week outdoors.

And among minority groups in urban areas, it only gets worse. Lack of green space, access to parks, and financial constraints mean children of color often have less access to wholesome outdoor activities.

This lack of outdoor exposure means a decreased understanding of the environment and the need to protect it.

Outreach to underserved populations is a major focus of *The Fishing Foundation*. We bring education directly to children who otherwise might not have access to environmental education opportunities. When children are exposed to educational programs and activities like fishing, they realize the importance of protecting the natural environment and essentially function as stewards of nature in their communities.

Spending time outdoors not only builds a respect for the environment, but it can also provide life long benefits as well. Connecting with green space such as parks and forests, and blue space, places with rivers and lakes, has been shown to help people get more exercise, reduce stress, build self-esteem, and overall improve a person's quality of life.

In addition, spending time outdoors isn't all just fun and games. People make careers working outdoors while making a positive impact on the environment. From tending the land and water, to protecting animals and wildlife, careers include conservationist,

Gail Ann Grizzell

scientist, forester, wildlife biologist, farmer, park ranger, and environmentalist.

By producing this book, we are taking the next step in our mission to enhance people's lives through the sport of fishing. Contained in these pages are instructions, tips and illustrations about the fundamentals of fishing, and important information about conservation and protecting the environment. This easy-to-read manual is designed as an educational tool and resource to enhance the hands-on experience.

Acknowledgments

THIS BOOK IS THE manifestation of our love of fishing and a desire to introduce youth to a sport that can create a lifetime of positive memories. It is our hope that this fishing manual will be a catalyst for beginning anglers as they develop an interest in the sport as well as a handy reference tool for use in the future.

John M. Hairston, award-winning educator and community activist, and Terry J. Cosby, state conservationist, Ohio Office, Natural Resources Conservation Service, USDA, are staunch supporters of our vision and are responsible for bringing this project to fruition. Thanks to John and Terry, thousands of children from Cleveland-area neighborhoods have participated in and benefited from fishing workshops and hands-on instruction held at local parks and campgrounds.

We are delighted that Becky's Graphic Design assisted us in publishing this book. A sincere and heartfelt word of appreciation to Becky Bayne, founder of Becky's Graphic Design®, LLC, and her team. Conversations and discussions with them have been invaluable in bringing this project to completion.

Over the past year, many people have volunteered their time and talent in support of this project. As a veteran journalist, Carrie Wise was instrumental in editing the initial manuscript. Ann Marie Gorman, fisheries biologist, Division of Wildlife, Ohio Division of Natural Resources, Fairport Fisheries Station also weighed in with words of encouragement, guidance, and meaningful comments. John Farson, aquatic education coordinator, Division of Wildlife, Ohio Division of Natural Resources also provided advice and counsel.

Many thanks to The Fishing Foundation's leadership, volunteers, sponsors, grant-makers, in-kind supporters, individual donors, and community partners who championed and supported our vision for educating youth about the joys of fishing and who through their time and treasure have sustained the organization's mission. A special thanks to graphic artist Jen Juan, owner of Maykah Designs, who worked with us from the inception of the nonprofit to create The Fishing Foundation's logo.

Past and current sponsors and funders include Cabela's, Cleveland Metroparks, Executive Meeting Planners, LLC, Murphy Family Foundation, Neighborhood Leadership Development Program, Northeast Ohio Regional Sewer District, Ohio Division of Natural Resources, Ohio Office, Natural Resources Conservation Service, USDA, RPM International Inc., Synthomer, the S. K. Wellman Foundation, Rhea of Hope Foundation, George H.W. Bush Vamos A Pescar™ Education Fund, and Walmart.

Individual donors include Karen Allan, Barbara M. Caves, Bonnie Fraser, Gary A. Grizzell, Gay A. Grizzell, Judy Suckno, and Beverly J. Thompson.

Partnerships and in-kind support include the Urban League of Greater Cleveland, the Cleveland Kids' Book Bank, Gift Guru, City of East Cleveland, City of Cleveland, Flambeau, New Horizon Bakery, North Coast Bass Anglers Association, Rainey Institute, and the Louis Stokes Cleveland VA Medical Center.

List of volunteers, including past and current board members: Alvenia Rhea Albright, Kathy Allen, Michael Bacon, John Ban, Debra Kee, Sandra Kay Boyd, Evelyn Knowles, Bob Davis, Gay A. Grizzell, Gary A. Grizzell, Nancy Hines, Patty Mack, Heidi McDaniel, Sylvester McDaniel Jr., Sylvester McDaniel, Tyler Boyd-Rosten, Kathy Sekerak, Donna Quayle, Joe Premura, and Jack Wallingford.

CONTENTS

Introduction

THE BEST THING ABOUT fishing is that anyone can do it!

Whether you're short, tall, shy, athletic or not, with practice and patience anyone can learn how to fish. *Learn to Fish: A Step-by-Step Guide for Beginning Anglers* was created as an instruction manual for anyone who wants to learn how to fish or become a better angler. Fishing is one of the most popular sports in the world. It's more popular than golf, soccer, and tennis. In the United States, approximately 50 million people take part in the sport of fishing every year, but it's much more than just a simple outdoor activity. There's the fun and excitement of preparing your tackle, packing a lunch, going over your checklist, buying bait, and traveling to your favorite body of water. Fishing teaches patience, time management skills, how to handle success and failure, and provides a sense of accomplishment and an appreciation for the great outdoors.

The goal of this book is to encourage a lifelong appreciation of the sport of fishing and to spark an appreciation for the great outdoors. Contained in *Learn to Fish: A Step-by-Step Guide for Beginning Anglers* are easy to follow instructions and illustrations that cover everything from water safety, setting up a rod and reel, and casting to information about fish habitats, fishing regulations, and finding the best areas to fish.

Throughout this book, you will also find some pro tips that are worth reading and remembering as well as personal stories about fishing from the authors. Getting started is simple, easy, and not all that expensive. Just remember, anyone can learn to fish!

THE HISTORY OF FISHING

The practice of catching fish for food dates back some 40 to 50 thousand years. At the time, it consisted of catching fish by hand or using simple tools like a spear, net, and trap. Native Americans fished with stones in the shape of hooks attached to homemade lines. Some tribes were even known to use toxins in streams to immobilize fish to capture them.

African Americans also have a long history of fishing, which in this country, dates back to 1619 when they were forcibly brought to what would become the United States. As slaves, they worked the land for their masters and harvested the seas, lakes, and streams to put food on the table for their families and others.

Enterprising slaves and free Blacks could also capitalize on their fishing skills by selling their catch or using it to barter for other goods. For slave owners, the act of fishing did not pose a threat because it didn't require the use of a weapon that could be turned against them.

As African Americans' fishing skills grew, so did new opportunities. Many found jobs along the major waterways building boats, casting nets for **shad** and other species, trimming sails on schooners and sloops, shoveling coal in fire rooms on steamships, and eventually becoming known as watermen. After the Civil War, more and more free Blacks found work along coastal waterways like the Potomac River and Chesapeake Bay.

The history of recreational fishing is not clear, but there is evidence of fly-fishing in Japan and Europe dating back as early as the ninth century. In 1496, the first documented evidence of sport fishing appeared in an essay on recreational angling published in England. English settlers brought the sport of fly-fishing to the United States in the early 1800s. Within a few decades, recreational fishing for trout had firmly taken root. Today, bass fishing has become the most popular game fish in the United States. Bass is a hearty, edible species that can withstand the cooler waters of northern states and warm southern waters.

Today, according to "Take Me Fishing, Special Report on Fishing," over 50 million Americans, or 17 percent of the U.S. population went fishing at least once. Of that number, approximately 8 in 10 were white, 9 percent Hispanic, and 8 percent were African American. Of the total participants, nearly 18 percent were women.

As you begin your journey to learn how to fish, remember that fishing is a way of enjoying the great outdoors and spending time with family and friends. In fact, an overwhelming majority of people who currently fish actually started as children. It's also worth remembering that catching a fish is not the most important aspect of the sport. What truly matters are the life lessons that come from that act of fishing and the experiences that will stay with you forever.

The Fishing Foundation volunteers and attendees fishing from shore.

CHAPTER 1

Fishing Safety

FISHING IS A FUN and relaxing activity that can be enjoyed all of your life. It's important to remember that because it takes place on the water and some special equipment is used, fishing can be dangerous. That's why it's necessary to follow some basic safety tips.

Ring Buoy

Life Jacket

Young, beginning fishermen, commonly known as anglers, should never go fishing by themselves and should always go with an adult. If an accident, like falling or slipping into the water happens, an adult can help. Always remember that if someone does fall into the water, you should not jump in and risk drowning. Throw them a life jacket or other personal flotation device (**PFD**) as these objects are designed to float in the water. As a last resort, you can use a rope or long stick to pull them to shore. If a boat is available, row out to them and pull them out of the water. If none of these options are available, immediately seek help.

A Trip Down Memory Lane with Dennis

I was 12 years old when I first went fishing along the shores of the Mississippi River in Wisconsin. It was a family affair with my mother, father, sister, uncle, and cousins. On most of our fishing outings, we would pitch tents and camp out overnight. Everyone would fish all day, and then we would cook out and sleep along the river. Our trips were about so much more than just going to fish. They were a time to be with family. Over the years, I became more involved in the planning of our trips and became a better angler as well. I grew to love fishing so much that I took my rods and reels to college so I could fish on the weekends. I still fish to this day, and I am a longtime member of a bass fishing club in Cleveland, Ohio.

WHAT TO WEAR

Whether you're fishing in hot or cold weather, it's important to protect your head, hands, legs, feet, and skin from the sun, cold, and rain. If it's sunny, make sure to apply sunscreen and wear a hat to protect your skin from the sun's harmful rays.  It's also a good idea to wear sunglasses to shield your eyes from the sunlight as it's even brighter when it reflects off of the water. Sunglasses will also hinder stray objects from getting into your eyes. You may also want to consider wearing long pants to guard against getting injured by the barb of a hook and closed-toe shoes to protect your feet.

ADDITIONAL SAFETY TIPS

LOOK BEFORE YOU CAST: Before you cast, take a second to make sure you're standing the length of the rod, or several feet, apart from other people. Then look behind you and from side-to-side, so you don't hit someone with the rod, hook, or other lures.

REMEMBER YOUR LIFE JACKET: If you're in a boat, you should always wear a life jacket, also known as a personal flotation device or a PFD, which is specially designed to strap on to you and help you float in the water.

SLIPPERY WHEN WET: When you're fishing from shore, a dock, or a landing, watch your footing! Rocks and logs can be very slippery when they are wet. If you're walking on a pier or along the shore of a lake or pond, be careful not to slip and fall in the water.

HANDLE HOOKS WITH CARE: Fishing hooks have a barb at the end that is very sharp. Be very careful not to hook yourself or someone else. You should always pay attention as you handle your hooks and use caution while tying them onto your line, putting on bait, removing the hook from the mouth of a fish, and when casting. We'll explain more about the uses and features of hooks in an upcoming chapter.

TACKLE THOSE TANGLES: If your fishing line becomes tangled or snagged, do not yank it. Pulling on it will only make it worse. Instead, find the area where the line is tangled and try to untie it. If that doesn't work, have someone cut the line for you and then retie the fishing tackle that was cut off.

LEAVE NO TRACE: Don't litter or leave your fishing line, sinkers, hooks, lures, or other items on the ground or in the water. If you can, safely remove them from the water and throw them away in a trash receptacle. It's important to keep the water and surrounding areas clean from trash to protect the environment. In addition, items left in the water or along the shoreline might be harmful to the fish, insects, or animals that live in the water or drink from it. We want to keep them safe, so always remove your trash from the area.

WATCH FOR SEVERE WEATHER: Severe weather such as a thunderstorm is dangerous. If a storm approaches, leave immediately and seek shelter in a sturdy building or car. Do not shelter under a tree. Lightening may be in the area and could reach you.

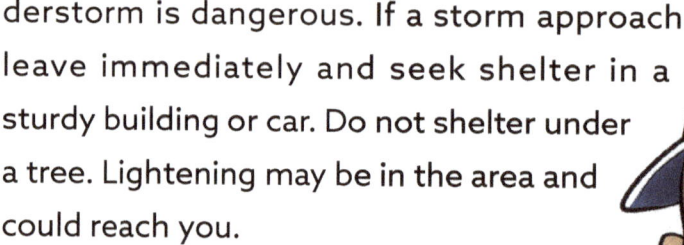

A Trip Down Memory Lane

USE CAUTION when fishing around rocks, wood surfaces like docks, and even concrete surfaces. On one outing, I was fishing along the Mississippi River with Uncle Ulysses. He hooked a nice fish, and we were all excited. He stepped onto some wet rocks along the shoreline to land the fish, but he was paying more attention to the fish than to his feet. He stepped on a patch of slippery moss, lost his footing, and fell. Fortunately, he wasn't hurt. Unfortunately, he lost his fish.

Uncle Ulysses

CHAPTER 2

All About Fish

IN THIS SECTION, WE'LL look at fish anatomy: how they eat, how they breathe, and even how they swim.

In the United States, there are approximately 800 species of fish. Every species of fish is unique. They're different in size, shape, length, and weight. Some fish prefer to live in murky, warm, calm lakebeds, while others thrive in clear, cold, fast-moving streams. Although there are some very interesting and unusual exceptions, most of the fish that anglers catch share many common traits. They live in water. They have a backbone. Most have scales. They have gills, fins, and a tail. They have the ability to see under water, smell, taste, hear, and feel. Almost all fish are cold-blooded, which means their body temperature changes as the water temperature changes. A fish's metabolism tends to speed up in warmer water

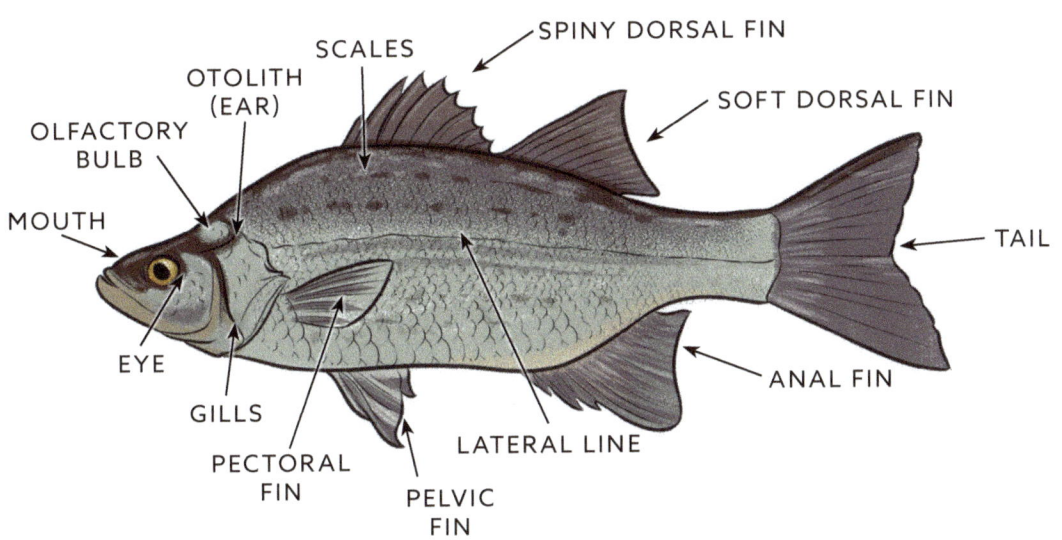

SPINY DORSAL FIN

SCALES

OTOLITH (EAR)

SOFT DORSAL FIN

OLFACTORY BULB

MOUTH

TAIL

EYE

ANAL FIN

GILLS

PECTORAL FIN

LATERAL LINE

PELVIC FIN

and slow down in colder water. In fact, water temperature plays a very important part in how active fish are. We'll learn more details about this later.

HOW FISH BREATHE

Gills enable a fish to breathe by removing oxygen from the water. The gills are located on both sides of the fish. You should never put your hand inside the gills or the gill cover when you handle a fish. If a fish cannot breathe, it cannot survive.

HOW FISH MOVE

The fins and tail allow fish to move left, right, up, down, and even backwards. Most fish swim less than two miles an hour, but they can reach speeds of 12 to 20 miles per hour in short bursts while still maintaining the ability to quickly change direction. Big fish generally swim faster than smaller fish.

HOW FISH SEE

A fish's ability to see under water is one of its most important senses. They have a protective film over their eyes to help them see clearly. As light enters the fish's eye, it's converted into an electric impulse which allows the optic nerve to relay the information to the brain to produce an image. Most species of fish have eyes on the side of their head allowing them to see objects to the left and right of their snout. They also see objects well above their head and slightly below it. Since their eyes are on the side of their head, most fish have somewhat of a blind spot when they're looking straight ahead.

Most fish also have sensors in their eyes that allow them to see color. In clear water, anglers often choose lure colors that match the main food source present in the lake to attract fish. In stained, low visibility waters, anglers opt for colors like white, chartreuse, pink, black, and dark blues that will contrast with cloudy water. Another great choice in these conditions is to use lures that create movement and noise. In addition to detecting color, fish see light and dark shades of gray, and most species have some level of night vision.

Biologists tell us that fish have excellent close-up vision but rather poor distance vision. The distance that fish see also depends on the condition of the water that day. Murky water conditions and, generally, deeper water conditions reduce the distance a fish can see. Some fish are also sensitive to bright light and look for habitats that provide shade on a sunny day.

Angler Advice from Miss Margaret

On bright sunny days, fish often seek shaded areas to avoid the sun. Large rocks, trees, brush piles, stumps, tall grass, docks, and other objects in the water are great places to fish. In addition, fish seek covered areas because they provide protection from predators. Cover also provides a place from which fish can launch attacks on unsuspecting prey. On cloudy days, anglers may find fish roaming in waters that are more open. These are areas worth targeting.

Miss Margaret

HOW FISH HEAR

Fish rely on their hearing to survive. Sound travels much better under water than through the air. Many fish receive sound through ear bones, also known as **otoliths**, located inside their head. They also feel sound vibrations in the water on both sides of their body through something called a lateral line. A lateral line is a series of cells on or just below the skin composed partially of hair cells that detect motion and water flow. The lateral line allows fish to sense the movement of other creatures, like fish, frogs, and insects, in the water. Together, the ear bones and the lateral line allow fish to hunt for food and avoid predators.

Did You Know?

Many artificial lures, such as *spinner baits*, buzz baits, top water baits, crank baits, and dozens of others, use sound as a way to attract fish and get them to bite. Anglers often add rattles that make a knocking noise to their lures to attract fish.

HOW FISH SMELL AND TASTE

The senses of taste and smell are closely related, but they perform different roles. For a fish to smell, water enters its nostrils and comes in contact with something called the **olfactory bulb.** This area transmits smell information from the nose to the brain allowing fish to detect possible sources of food such as wounded or distressed creatures, including crawfish, minnows, and frogs. Fish only taste after something enters their mouth. They taste through the same olfactory bulb used for smell. If something feels and tastes like food, they hold onto it. If not, they let go.

Did You Know?

Fish use their sense of smell during mating, hunting, and feeding. For this reason, many anglers use artificial scents that they spray or rub on lures to help attract fish.

MORE ABOUT THE LATERAL LINE

Some fish, like bass, feel vibrations from objects in the water through a sensory organ of hair cells that runs along the length of a fish known as a lateral line. These hair cells detect movement, sound vibrations, and pressure changes in surrounding waters. Fish use their lateral line to locate prey and escape predators. Although a fish's ability to see and hear are most important, sensing food or predators with the lateral line is very helpful to a fish when the sun is very bright or when the water is too dark or too murky for fish to see.

WHAT FISH EAT

After fish eggs hatch they are called larvae, and they have a small sac attached to them that provides them with food and nutrition. As the young fish grow, their mouths begin to develop, and they no longer rely on the egg sac as a food source. This is known as the fry stage. The fry begin to feed on their own—eating small creatures like tiny crustaceans or *zooplankton* (organisms that float in the water that are so small they are not visible to the naked eye). When fish get a little bigger, they begin to eat insects, plants, larvae, grasshoppers, smaller fish, worms, frogs, crayfish, and leeches.

Did You Know?

All of these make great baits.

Night Crawlers   *Minnow*   *Wax Worms*   *Crawfish*

Fish are either active (hungry) feeders, neutral (not hunting, but will feed), or inactive (not hungry), but most fish will not pass up an easy meal.

When fish are actively feeding, they are easier to catch. Their feeding area and the distance they will travel for a meal has a wide range—several feet or more. Fish will move away from the security of shelter, like downed trees, rocks, and grass, and will swim into open water in order to feed. The area directly in front of a fish and the areas to the left and right of its snout are prime hunting areas. They also see objects well above their head and slightly below it.

Did You Know?

Fish often feed in the early morning and at dusk. This is partially because during sunrise and sunset light levels are lower. As noted earlier, many species are sensitive to bright light and are therefore more likely to look for a meal while the sun is not high in the sky.

When fish are in a neutral state, they are not actively hunting, but they will feed if the opportunity presents itself, like if a vulnerable prey moves into the area. When fish are in an inactive state, they are not in the mood to eat so your bait must be near enough, perhaps even right in their face, to draw a **strike**.

Fish feed for different reasons. If an easy meal is presented, chances are they will eat it. After feeding, chances are they will not feed again while digesting their food. Water temperature can also affect fish feeding patterns. Generally, their metabolism slows in the winter when water temperatures drop below 40 degrees Fahrenheit. Because they do not use a lot of energy, they do not need to eat as much. As the water warms to 65 degrees Fahrenheit and above, fish become more active. They require more food and may expand their feeding area. You may think fish would eat more in the summer when the water is warmest; however, this is not always the case. During summer months, the water may become too warm for some fish, and they may slow down and move deeper seeking cooler water. Feeding in the fall tends to increase again as they prepare for a long, cold winter when their metabolism slows down.

Fish that rely on their sight for food are affected by water clarity and light. If a fish is sensitive to bright light, it may prefer to feed in less clear water or in the early morning and evening.

HOW FISH FEED

The way fish feed varies by species. One common way that fish hunt is by chasing down their prey. Many species of fish can run down slower moving sources of food. Some fish, such as catfish and carp, are scavengers. They eat dead or dying objects that fall to the bottom of the lake. Other fish feed by stalking their prey. They do this by slowly moving closer to their prey without frightening it, and then with a burst of speed, they attack. Ambushing their prey is a method of lying in wait for a source of food to get close enough for the fish to lunge forward and strike at its food.

Some fish species capture their prey by opening their mouths and expanding their gills, creating a powerful vacuum. Water, and the food they're after, are sucked into their mouths. The excess water is pushed out through the gills.

Did You Know?

When fishing with live bait or artificial lures, anglers should experiment with different fishing patterns, such as fishing on the bottom, fishing near the surface, moving your bait gingerly through the water, letting the bait sit still in the water, and using different baits or lures.

Uncle Ulysses's Fishing Wisdom

When fishing, if you feel movement of your line or see it suddenly jump, it probably means that a fish has inhaled your bait, and you should set the hook. Setting the hook is the act of planting the hook into the mouth of a fish. To do so, when you feel the weight of a fish on the line, point your rod tip toward the water and reel up the slack in the line. In one quick motion, bring the rod tip up to the 12 o'clock position forcing the hook into the mouth of the fish.

All fish have some form of teeth. We may not think of them as having teeth because they come in many different forms, and they are located in different places within a fish's mouth. Carnivores, or meat-eating fish, have more canine-like teeth for grabbing, holding, and grinding down their prey. Plant-eaters, or herbivores, may have teeth you cannot easily see that are located in the back of their throat or molded together as one large unit used to break down plants.

A BIT ABOUT BAIT

Fishing with live bait allows you to catch a wide variety of fish. The food, or bait, can include plants, insects, larvae, grasshoppers, smaller fish, such as minnows, worms, frogs, crayfish, leeches, and man-made baits. There are three favorite types of live bait that many anglers use: earthworms (also called night crawlers), wax worms (a small, off-white variety of moth larvae measuring about 1 inch in length), and minnows (a family of small fish, mainly in the carp family).

Earthworms work well for catching bluegill, sunfish, largemouth bass, catfish, and other fish species. Putting the entire worm on the hook is not necessary. In most cases, only use one-half or one-third so the bait will not come off during casting or when a fish bites. Putting a smaller piece of a worm on the hook is just as effective as using the entire worm. It also helps prevent the fish from pulling away the entire worm. Store your night crawlers in a cool, dry place to help keep them alive.

To securely attach a worm, thread a good portion of the worm about 1 inch up the hook. Then bring the hook out the side of the worm exposing the hook. Be careful: hooks are sharp.

Another technique is to place the hook through the middle of the worm exposing the hook. The barb on the hook will keep the worm from slipping off.

Wax worms work well for catching bluegill, crappies, and sunfish. Carefully attach a wax worm using the same method as above. Hook them through the middle or run the hook up the center and expose the hook.

Minnows are an excellent choice for catching crappie, large-mouth bass, white bass, perch, walleye, and a variety of other fish. Minnows work best when they are alive. They should be kept in a bucket with fresh, cool water. Often anglers purchase inexpensive air pumps that run on batteries and attach to the side of a bucket. These pumps drive oxygen into the water to help keep your fish alive. Anglers typically attach minnows in one of two ways: through the lips exposing the hook or through the center of the body exposing the hook.

The Fishing Foundation volunteers assembling rods and reels.

WARNING:

Whether it is dead or alive, do not dispose of bait into the water. Doing so can spread a new disease or cause a new species to disrupt the ecosystem. You should dispose of bait in the garbage or find a way to preserve it for another day of fishing.

A boy and a night crawler.

CHAPTER 3

Fishing Equipment

FISHING RODS AND REELS

In this section, we discuss some basic fishing equipment and how to use it. Going fishing does not require top-of-the-line, expensive equipment to get started, catch fish, or have a good time. The two most essential pieces of equipment are a rod and a reel. They often come together in a set but are sold separately as well.

The reel is the device that holds your fishing line. Most reels do not come with line on them, so you may have to purchase it. The three most common types of reels are spincast, spinning, and baitcast. Reels hold about 100 yards of line. We'll discuss the three varieties of reels in more detail later.

Angler Advice from Miss Margaret

Consider changing your fishing line at the start of each fishing season. Line that sits on your reel for extended periods may become brittle and twisted. This may cause your line to break or become knotted. Line used last season may have become nicked or stretched and may break.

A rod is a long shaft made from graphite, fiberglass, or other composite materials. The handle is found at the end of the rod, the thickest part of the rod and where you hold it with your dominant hand when casting. Along the length of the rod are guides, also referred to as **eyes**, that the fishing line is strung through.

Rods come in different lengths, power (size or thickness), and action (where the rod bends) from ultra-light to ultra-heavy. Generally, light rods are used when fishing for smaller fish, and heavy rods are used when fishing for bigger fish.

PRO TIP:

A medium power, 5- to 6-foot-long rod is a good all-around rod for beginners. Some rods and reels are sold together, but most are sold separately.

SPINCAST REEL (CLOSED-FACE REEL)

A **spincast reel** is an inexpensive, simple to use outfit and is ideal for beginners. It's sometimes called a closed-face reel because the line is spooled around a drum located behind the closed-face part of the reel. To properly use a spincast reel, the reel should always face up. Grip the handle with your casting hand, and securely hold the button on the top of the reel down with your thumb. It's important to maintain pressure on the button throughout the entire cast. Next, bring the rod over your shoulder, behind your head, and then forward all in one quick motion. As the rod moves forward and toward your target, let the button go to release the line. The line is taken up by turning the handle that rotates a drum inside the closed face of the reel.

SPINNING REEL

A *spinning reel* has an open face and is designed to operate with the reel hanging below the rod. The line is exposed and wrapped around a cylinder called a spool. The line is taken up by turning a handle that rotates a thick wire arm in front of the spool. This arm is called a bail, and it is referred to as open or closed when it is flipped up or down. As the bail turns, it takes up the line and wraps it around the spool. When the bail is down, or closed, it stops line from coming off the reel. When the bail is open, or flipped up, fishing line can come off the spool.

To cast with this type of reel, begin with the bail closed. Then, grip the handle with your casting hand and hold the line with the tip of your index finger. With your other hand, open the bail. While continuing to hold the line with your index finger, bring the rod over your shoulder and behind your head. In one quick motion, bring the rod forward in the direction of your target and let go of the line by lifting your index finger off the line. To reel the line in, use your other hand to turn the handle. This will automatically close the bail and wind the line.

PRO TIP:

Most spinning reels allow you to easily switch the reel handle from one side of the reel to the other depending on which side you prefer. To do this, unscrew the dust cap on the side of the reel and unscrew the handle on the opposite side of the reel. Then, insert the arm handle in the other side and replace the dust cover. That's it! You switched the handle from one side to the other.

BAITCAST REEL

A **baitcast reel** mounts on top of the rod. The line is spooled around a drum that spins around when you rotate the handle. To cast, grip the handle with your casting hand and push down the release button while at the same time placing your thumb on the drum to hold the line in place. In one quick motion, bring the rod behind your head, then forward, and ease your thumb off of the drum, allowing the line to spool out while maintaining enough pressure to slow your bait or lure down to prevent tangling. Beginners may find this rod difficult to use and should practice before fishing with it.

DRAG SETTING

Most reels have a drag adjustment. Setting it properly is essential. If your drag is too tight, the line may snap if a fish runs. If it's too loose, when you try to reel in the line, it will not spool onto the reel.

The drag adjustment is typically a small dial located on the front, top, or side of the reel. Turning this dial allows you to set how much resistance there is when pulling line off the reel. You want to set the resistance based on the strength of the line, also known as the *pound test*, or the amount of pounds of pressure the line can withstand before breaking.

The higher the pound test, the stronger the line. A properly set drag is tight enough so that if a fish tries to dart away, the line will pull off the spool. Then as the fish tires and begins to stop fighting, the proper drag setting will allow you to take up line and reel the fish in.

ABOUT FISHING RODS

There are hundreds of rods made of different materials that are tailored for specific species of fish. They come in different lengths and thicknesses that match every type of reel on the market. In this section, we'll cover rod power, action, and length.

Power describes a rod's strength and resistance to bending. It is classified as ultra-light, light, medium-light, medium, medium-heavy, heavy, or ultra-heavy. Usually, the power of a rod is matched to the type of fishing you're doing, the species you're fishing for, or the size of fish you're after. For example, a light rod is suitable for catching pan fish, an assortment of smaller fish such as bluegills, pumpkin-seeds, crappie, white bass, and yellow perch, while a medium rod is more suitable for bass and larger fish. A medium rod is a general, all-purpose rod. A heavy rod is generally used with heavy fishing line, like 20-pound test and stronger, and when fishing around thick cover where fish burrow into the weeds. A stiff rod with heavy line is needed to hoist fish from these weeded areas.

Action refers to where the rod bends when weight is applied to it. Rod action may be slow, medium, fast, or anything in between (e.g., medium-fast). The action will influence how far an angler can cast, the responsiveness when a fish takes a hook, and the action felt when reeling the fish in. A fast tip rod bends more at the tip. A slower rod bends closer to the handle. Generally, a fast tip rod will give a firmer hook set after a fish takes your bait than a slower action rod. It will also cast lures farther than a slow-action rod and provide more control of the fish when reeling it in.

SLOW ACTION: This type of rod bends more toward the butt (handle) of the rod. It is the most flexible.

MEDIUM/MODERATE ACTION: This type of rod bends toward the middle of the shaft. It's a bit more flexible than a fast-action rod.

FAST ACTION: For this type of rod, most of the bend happens toward the tip of the rod.

ROD LENGTH

Fishing rods come in various lengths ranging from approximately 5 to 7.6 feet. The length of the rod along with the material it is made from will have an effect on the power and action of the rod. Generally, long rods cast farther than shorter rods. The additional length allows the rod to load up with more line and power to cast farther. A long length rod also provides more leverage when reeling in a fish.

PARTS OF THE ROD

HANDLE: The handle is where you hold the rod. Often called the grip, handles come in a variety of materials, including foam, cork, plastic, or a composite material.

CAP OR BUTT: The end of the rod handle, called the cap or butt, is often made of plastic to protect the bottom end of the rod.

SEAT: This is the place where the reel attaches to the rod. Most seats have a socket where the reel sits. The reel is held in place by a screw ring, called a hood, that goes over the foot of the reel.

HOOK KEEPER: A small, simple loop of metal, usually above the seat, the hook keeper is used to slip your hook through to prevent your line and hook from swinging about when not being used.

GUIDES OR EYES: These are the rings along the shaft of the rod. They guide the line down the length of the rod. The number of guides, the material they're made of, their spacing, and their size vary depending on the quality and type of the rod. Generally, the more guides the better the rod. Better rods will have at least one guide per foot. A 6-foot rod should have at least six guides.

WINDINGS: Windings are what hold the guides in place. They are usually made of string that's wrapped around the foot of the guide and painted over with enamel to protect it from wear and tear and to prevent it from moving.

FERRULE (FAIR-EL): If you have a two-piece rod, the ferrule is the joint where the larger and smaller sections fit together.

ROD TIP: The last guide at the end of your fishing rod. It is the smallest, and most important. It is also the easiest to break off. Take care.

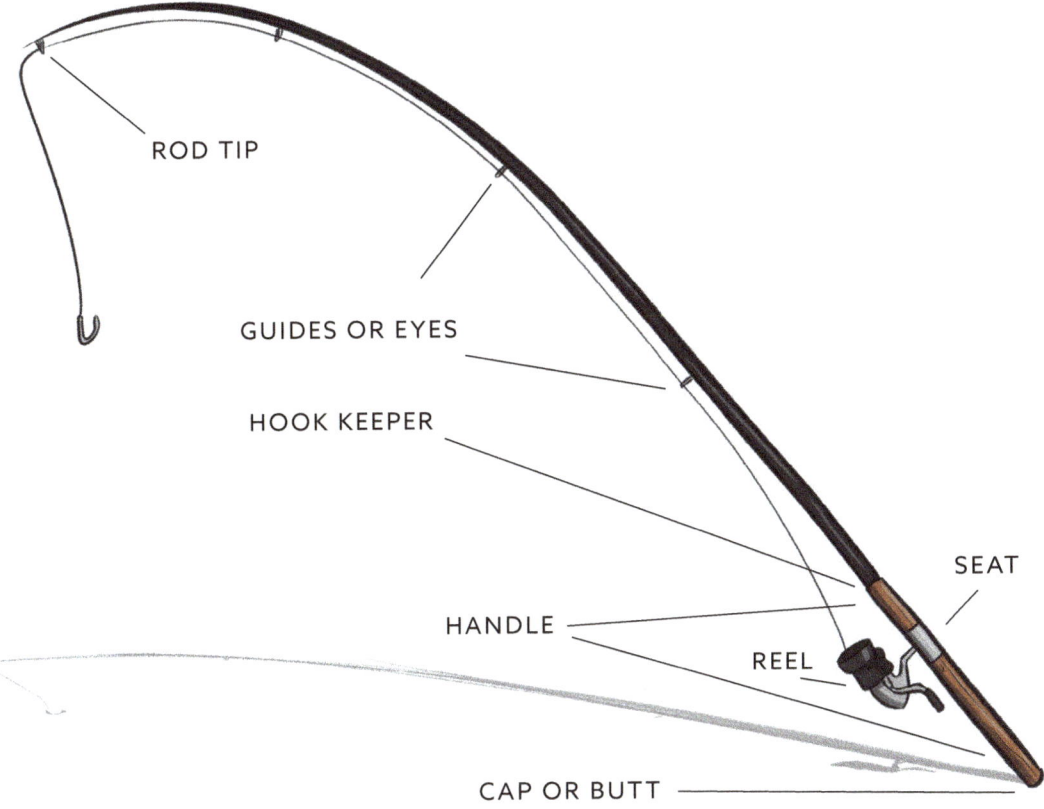

ROD TIP

GUIDES OR EYES

HOOK KEEPER

HANDLE

REEL

SEAT

CAP OR BUTT

PRO TIP:

Many rods list information and specifications about the rod near the handle. You should see the length of the rod, the action, the recommended lure size, and the line size that is suited for that rod. For beginning anglers, a good, all-around rod to consider is a 5- to 6-foot, medium-action rod.

A family affair, granddad takes his grandkids fishing.

CHAPTER 4

Fishing Line

FISHING LINE

Every reel requires some sort of fishing line to be spooled on it—usually somewhere between 75–100 yards of line. The line should come up to about an eighth of an inch below the top of the spool. If too much line is put on the spool, the line will come off too quickly and tangle, or **backlash**.

Fishing line is rated by the amount of weight, or strength, it will hold before it breaks. This is commonly referred to as pound test. You may see 10-pound test printed on the package, for example. This means the line will withstand 10 pounds of pressure before it snaps. Generally, fishing line will withstand more pressure than what it is rated. There are several different types of fishing line. Three of the most common are monofilament, braid, and fluorocarbon. Let's look at each of these in more detail.

MONOFILAMENT FISHING LINE

Monofilament line, also known simply as *mono* is made from plastic. It's usually clear, but also comes in other colors. It is relatively buoyant and sinks slowly in the water. What quality anglers like about mono is its ability to stretch a bit, so it will not snap when a fish first takes your lure or bait and darts off. It is usually the least expensive of the three types of line, very durable, and a good all-around line to use. It's a good choice for beginning anglers.

BRAID FISHING LINE

Braid fishing line is a man-made, fiber-like line that is popular with anglers because of its strength and resistance to stretching. Generally, it's used to fish around heavy cover, like rocks, timber, bushes, and other objects. Although braid line floats in the water, thanks to its thin diameter, it also cuts through the water column and allows the lure to fall and run deep. Because it does not stretch, braid line is very sensitive. When a fish bites or moves your bait, that movement is transmitted through your line to your rod.

FLUOROCARBON FISHING LINE

Fluorocarbon line, also known as *fluoro*, is made from artificial materials including special plastics, nylon, and Dacron. Because fluoro is so dense, it sinks in the water. It also has very little stretch making it very sensitive to movement and able to hold up well to wear. Because fluoro has a thin diameter it is nearly invisible in the water, so it's a good choice when fishing in clear water. For all these reasons, it's become a popular choice of line.

PRO TIP:

For beginning anglers, 8-pound monofilament fishing line is a good choice. To reduce the harm to wildlife, remember to dispose of your line properly. Fishing line that is left on the shore or in the water can be eaten by fish and other animals or get tangled around birds, fish, or other creatures that live along the shoreline.

HOW TO LOAD FISHING LINE

Putting line on your rod correctly is extremely important. If it's put on incorrectly, there's a chance of getting a twist in your line. When this occurs, the line might coil instead of hanging limp, which may cause your line to tangle when you cast.

For beginners, it's easiest to have someone put your line on for you. Many sporting goods stores and tackle shops will put new line on for you at a minimal cost.

LOADING A SPINNING REEL

Follow these steps to load the line onto a spinning reel.

- Attach the reel to the rod. Place the fishing line from the manufacturer on the floor with the label facing up.
- Run the line through the first eye on your rod (the one closest to your reel).
- Open the bail (the wire arm in front of the spool that flips up and down).
- Wrap the line around the spool a couple of times, tie a simple overhand knot, and cut the extra line away from the knot.
- Close the bail.

LOADING A SPINNING REEL, *CONTINUED*

- Use your thumb and index finger to pinch the line and apply a bit of pressure to it.
- With your other hand, slowly turn the handle and begin loading the line. Maintain constant pressure on the line while loading it.
- After 10 to 12 cranks of the handle, check for line twist. To do this, let some slack line lay on the floor. If the loops look twisted onto themselves, your line is probably spooling in the wrong direction on your reel. To fix it, simply flip the spool so that the label side is down, and then finish spooling line on the reel until it's about an eighth of an inch from the top of your reel. If the slack line on the floor looks relaxed, continue spooling onto your reel. Do not over fill the spool; it will cause the line to come off too quickly when you cast. After you finish putting line on the reel, and with the bail still closed, pull an extra 10 feet of fishing line from the spool sitting on the floor.
- Thread the end of the line through all of the eyes on the rod.
- Finally, tie on your tackle or lure at the end of the line.

LOADING A SPINCASTER

Follow the steps below for putting line on a spincast reel.

- Attach the reel to the rod.
- Remove the housing that covers the reel by unscrewing it. Put the cover aside.
- Run the line through the first eye on your rod (the one closest to your reel).
- Wrap the line around the spool a couple of times, tie a simple overhand knot, and cut off the extra line away from the knot.
- Lay the spool of line from the manufacturer face up on the floor and use the handle on the reel to begin loading line.
- After 10 to 12 cranks, check for line twist. If line twist is occurring, flip the spool face down and continue loading the line.
- Fill the spool on the reel to about an eighth of an inch from the top of your reel. Do not over fill the spool; it will cause the line to spill off.
- Leave an extra 10 feet of line at the end.
- Thread the line through the reel cover and screw it back in place.
- Put the line through all of the eyes on the rod.
- Finally, tie on your lure or bait at the end of the line.

LOADING A BAITCASTER

Follow the steps below to load the line onto a baitcaster for the first time.

- Attach the rod to the reel.
- Feed the line on the manufacturer's spool through the first eye on the rod (the one closest to the reel).
- Thread the line through the line guide on the reel.
- Loop the line around the drum two or three times, tie an overhand knot, and cut off the extra line.
- To make sure the line comes off the spool straight, put a pencil through the hole on the spool of line. Have a friend hold the pencil, or place it between your legs. It's easier than it sounds!
- Begin spooling the line while keeping a bit of pressure on it with your thumb and index finger.
- Don't over fill the spool. Leave about an eighth of an inch gap from the top.
- Leave some extra line at the end and feed it through all of the eyes on your rod.
- Finally, tie on your bait or lure.

CHAPTER 5

Other Equipment

SINKERS/WEIGHTS

Sinkers, also known as **weights**, are small pieces of metal designed to clip or tie onto your line. Weights help your bait, or lure, fall to the bottom of the lake or stay in place. When paired with a bobber, a device that floats in the water, a weight helps prevent the bobber from moving about. Some of the most common styles of weights are bullet weights, sinkers, and split-shots. Weights come in a variety of sizes from as small as a sixteenth of an ounce to 2 ounces.

Most weights are made of lead-based material. Because lead is considered hazardous to the environment, many anglers prefer using sinkers made from tungsten. Tungsten is denser than lead, so the weights are smaller and more expensive than lead sinkers.

PRO TIP:

An all-around, good purpose weight is a quarter-ounce sinker.

HOOKS

The fishing hook is one of the most well-known pieces of fishing equipment. Hooks come in a variety of sizes and shapes for different applications. They are extremely sharp, and care should be taken when tying them onto your line, when putting on bait, and when casting.

Every part of the hook has a name and specific purpose. For our purpose, we'll look at the two ends of a hook—the eye and the point.

The eye is the part of the hook where you tie your line. Eyes come in different designs. One of the most common is a round-shaped ring eye. This type of eye is easy to thread line through and works well with a variety of knots. At the other end of the hook is the point; there are a few different point shapes. Two of the most common are the needle and the spear. Needle shaped points taper slightly inward. They're designed to easily pierce the inner mouth of the fish causing minimum damage and reducing harm. Spear shaped points are the most common hooks. Spear points are straight and cause little damage to the fish. Another part of the point worth mentioning is the barb. It runs in the opposite direction of the point. The barb is used to keep your bait on the hook. It also helps prevent a fish from throwing your hook and coming loose.

Hooks come in different sizes. They are sorted in two different ways, which can lead to some confusion. Hook measurements are defined by number size, using the number (#) symbol, or by something called an *aught*, using the forward slash (/) symbol. The symbol will appear on the packaging of the hooks you're buying along with a number.

Hooks that use a number size begin with size #1, then #2, and continue by twos (#4, #6, #8, and so on). A hook with a smaller number, such as a #2, is actually larger than a hook with a greater number, like a size #8 hook.

Aught sized hooks are identified by a forward slash (/) and a number. For example, a three aught size hook is written as 3/0 and pronounced three aught. They start at size 1/0 and go up one number at a time (1/0, 2/0, 3/0, and so on). A 6/0 aught hook is larger than a 1/0 aught hook.

Aught (/) sized hooks and numbered (#) hooks both begin with a number one size hook. A 1/0 aught and #1 hook are about the same size. As numbered hooks go up, #2, #4, #6, etc., they become smaller. A #22 hook is much smaller than a #2 hook. The opposite is true for hooks arranged by aughts. As hook sizes go up, 1/0, 2/0, 3/0, etc., the hooks become larger. A 6/0 is larger than a 1/0.

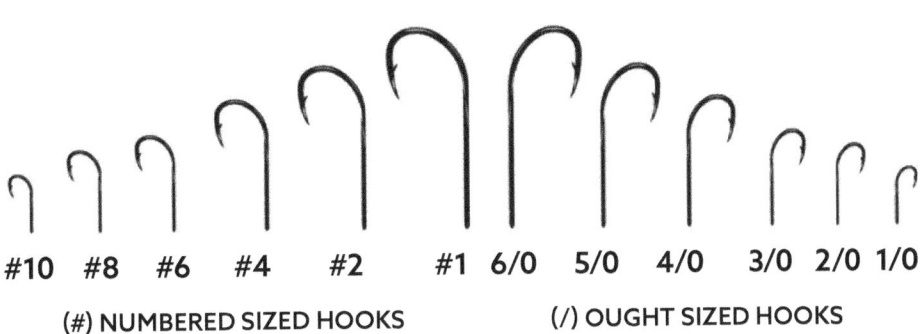

#10 #8 #6 #4 #2 #1 6/0 5/0 4/0 3/0 2/0 1/0

(#) NUMBERED SIZED HOOKS   (/) OUGHT SIZED HOOKS

PRO TIP:

A good hook for beginners is a bait holder hook. It has a barb near the point of the hook. A size #6 hook will work to catch a variety of fish species.

BOBBERS

A bobber is a small flotation device that sits on the surface of the water preventing your hook and weight from sinking to the bottom. Bobbers come in a variety of shapes and sizes and attach about 2 feet from the end of your line. Typically, you attach your sinker approximately 1 foot below the bobber. You tie your hook at the end of the line.

Bobbers let anglers know when they have a bite. Because your bobber floats on the surface, if it suddenly moves or is pulled under the water, there is a good chance that a fish has taken your bait. If you believe you have a bite, immediately set the hook (we will discuss setting the hook a bit later) and start reeling in your line. Make sure you try to keep your rod tip up at the two o'clock position as you reel.

PRO TIP:

When you get a bite, you do not have to reel in too fast. It's more important to focus on keeping the rod tip up and maintaining pressure on the fish. Do not allow slack in your line. If slack forms in your line, there's a good chance that the hook will come loose, and your fish will come off.

CHAPTER 6

How to Prepare before Going Fishing

THE MOST IMPORTANT THING to remember about going fishing is to have fun! It's a chance to spend time with friends and family and to enjoy the great outdoors. Getting started fishing is easy and does not have to be expensive.

THE BASIC ITEMS YOU'LL need are:

1. Ice inside a cooler with bottled water or soft drinks
2. Snacks and a lunch
3. Hat
4. Sunglasses
5. Camera
6. Sunscreen

THE BASIC ITEMS, CONTINUED

7. Fishing license, if required by your state

8. First aid kit

9. Raincoat

10. Pliers with a long nose to remove hooks

11. Hooks

12. Bobbers

13. Sinkers/weights

14. Life jacket

15. A stringer to attach your fish and keep them in the water

16. Rod and reel with fishing line

17. Tackle box to hold your equipment

18. Net

19. Bait

20. Bug spray

A Trip Down Memory Lane

When Gail was a child, preparing to go fishing was a family affair. The night before, granddad and grandma would make dough balls, a concoction made primarily of cornmeal, flour, garlic, water, and sometimes vanilla. They'd roll the dough into small balls about the size of a penny and boil them for a few minutes to make them firm. After that, they were dried and put into a bag in the refrigerator.

Gail's mom, Miss Margaret, would prepare the fishing equipment (she'd always add a colorful bobber to the cane poles), make lunches, and pack refreshments in the large blue and white cooler. Gail's father and brother would go to the neighborhood bait shop and buy a bucket full of live minnows, tiny silver-colored baitfish used to attract bigger fish. Gail's job was to gather earthworms. So, in the early evening, Gail and her sister would water the lawn with the garden hose to encourage the earthworms to come to the surface. Then she would pull out a flashlight to help find them easily. Once spotted, she would pull them from the ground and put them in a small, aerated container full of moist soil.

At the crack of dawn, the alarm clock would jolt them from their dreams. Thirty minutes later, with the cars packed, they were driving to the lake, and everyone was jokingly declaring they'd be the first to catch a fish. Gail always looked forward to days spent fishing; it meant having fun with family and making fond memories.

Miss Margaret

CHAPTER 7

Where to Fish

A Trip Down Memory Lane with Dennis:

I grew up fishing near large bodies of water like Lake Erie and the Mississippi River. My dad and uncle preferred to fish along rocky shorelines and rock walls, known as rip rap, because these areas always seemed to hold fish. As I gained more experience fishing, I learned why. Rocks hold heat and attract baitfish, crawfish, and other small creatures. With an abundant food source, larger fish are likely to show up.

SELECTING A PLACE TO FISH

As a beginning angler, fishing from shore is a great opportunity to improve your skills and gain valuable experience. Fishing from shore is a very different experience from fishing in a boat where you have access to the entire lake. If you are new to the sport, however, fishing from shore is less overwhelming and is a relatively safe, great place to get started.

Before going fishing, check with officials in your state to determine if you need a license to fish. After identifying a place to fish, confirm that you have permission to be on the property. Many public lakes have designated fishing areas set up for anglers to fish from. Some bodies of water have fish attractors in the water such as rock piles, timber, or other structures that provide a good habitat (shade, food, and cover) for fish. These can be great areas to target. Other areas to fish might come from the advice of family, friends, searching on the internet to learn about the lake, or checking with staff at a bait store in the area.

If it's your first time fishing on a body of water, try fishing around vegetation such as lily pads, grasses, and shrubs. Just be careful not to get your line hung up on the plant life. Other areas to

consider are fallen trees, logs in the water, docks, around bridges, and areas with plenty of rocks. These areas provide shade and shelter for small creatures and insects to live and grow. These breeding grounds attract small fish, which in turn attract larger fish. If fishing from shore, be mindful of getting your line caught when casting near trees or shrubs.

Mornings and late afternoons are often the best times of the day to fish. Because fish have eyes that are sensitive to light, they are more prone to roam bodies of water in search of food under these low-light conditions. If you're fishing when the sun is high in the sky, try fishing in shaded areas of the lake or in deeper water.

Keep in mind that just about any body of water will hold fish. The ideal location is a place with a healthy environment where the water is clean and has plenty of food, oxygen, and shelter. It's also worth mentioning that when fishing, probe the bottom of the water column and just under the surface. We'll explain how to fish the lake bottom and near the surface in the next chapter. Fish often come to the surface to feed on minnows and other small bait. At other times, fish hug the bottom in areas where vegetation grows.

As a reminder, if your state requires you to have a fishing license, pick that up ahead of time and have it with you when you arrive at your fishing spot. Then, prepare your gear and head out!

Casting a country mile.

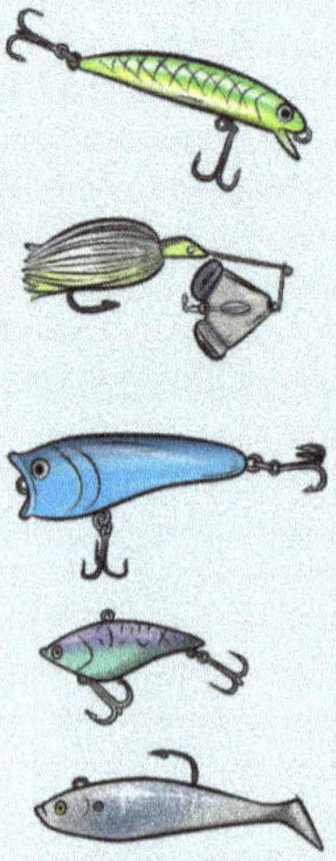

Lending a helping hand at a
Fishing Foundation event.

CHAPTER 8

How to Rig a Rod and Reel

RIGGING A ROD AND reel refers to the way you attach your fishing tackle—the hook, weight, bait, bobber, or lure—to your fishing line. There are many ways to rig (set up) a rod and reel. Two of the best ways that require very little expertise are utilizing a bobber and fishing directly on the bottom of the lake or body of water.

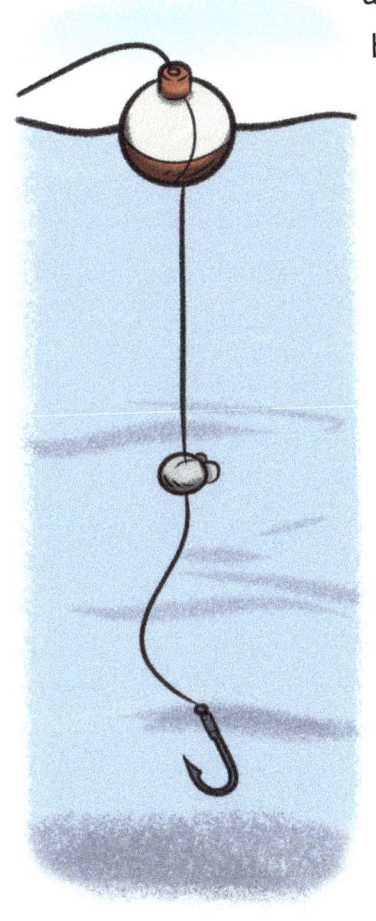

Before setting up either of these rigs, your reel should already have line spooled on it with the reel attached to the pole, and the line should be threaded through all of the eyes on your fishing pole. Leave about 5 feet of extra line at the end of the rod so you can set up the bottom and bobber rigs.

BOBBER RIG

The bobber rig is one of the most well-known rigs because of its versatility, easy setup, and ability to catch fish. With your reel attached to the rod and line threaded through all of the eyes on your pole, pull off approximately 5 feet of line and tie your hook on the end of your fishing line. (See How to Tie a Knot in the next chapter.) Next, attach a bobber of your choice approximately 2 feet above the hook. Remember, the bobber helps the line float. Then, about 1 foot above the hook, attach a sinker/weight. Look for weights that you can crimp onto your line using a pair of pliers. A good size weight to begin with is a quarter ounce or less. When you're finished, you should wind up with the hook at the end of your line, then a weight, and then a bobber. With this rig, you can easily adjust the position of the bobber by moving it up to fish deeper or sliding it lower on the line to fish shallow. Now, attach your bait to the hook and you're ready to fish!

After casting your line in the water, keep an eye on your bobber. When you see it pulled under the water or moving about, it means you might have a fish on the line. Set the hook and begin reeling in. If you miss the fish, cast again and enjoy.

BOTTOM RIG

Another easy setup is a bottom rig. As the name implies, this setup allows you to fish the bottom of a body of water. With your reel attached to the rod and line threaded through all of the eyes on your pole, pull off approximately 5 feet of line and tie a sinker/weight about 1 or 2 feet before the end of the line. (See How to Tie a Knot in the next chapter.) A half-ounce weight is a good size to begin with. Next, tie a hook onto the end of the line and attach your bait. What you should wind up with is the hook at the end of the line and a sinker about 1 to 2 feet above the hook. With this setup, when you cast into the water, your weight rests on the bottom of the lake, and your bait freely drifts in the current inches off the bottom.

A slightly different way of setting up a bottom rig is to attach a swivel to the end of your line. A fishing swivel is a small device made of two small metal rings connected in the middle by an oval-shaped joint that allows the two rings to pivot (rotate) independently of each other. With the swivel attached to the end of your line, cut 2 feet of fishing line (called a leader) and tie that to the bottom ring of the swivel. Next, attach your weight to the end of the leader. A half-ounce weight is a good size to begin with. At this point, you should have a weight at the end of your line with a swivel about 1 foot above the weight. The final step is to attach another piece of leader, about 1 foot long, to the swivel. At the end of that leader, attach a hook and then your bait. With this setup, your weight sits on the bottom and your bait sits about a foot off the bottom.

With either of the bottom rigs, you should allow the sinker to reach the bottom after you cast. Slowly reel in any slack until you begin to feel the weight, and then stop reeling. The bottom rig requires you to watch your line where it meets (enters) the water or watch the tip of your rod. If you see your line move, the tip of your rod jump, or feel something tugging on your rod, you may have a fish on the line. You should set the hook and begin reeling in.

SWIVEL

HOOK

1-2 FOOT LEADER

WEIGHT

A Trip Down Memory Lane

Miss Margaret was an avid angler. Her favorite way of fishing was on the bottom using minnows or night crawlers. In addition to this style of fishing, she taught us how to fish near the surface using a bobber. She'd put the fishing line on a cane pole and then added a bobber and a small hook with a worm on it. She tossed the line into the water and told me to watch the action of the bobber because if it dropped below the surface then we had a fish.

It was so exciting the first time we saw the bobber dip below the surface of the water. We'd squeal with joy and announce, "We're making contact!"

Miss Margaret smiled widely and said, "That's good!"

As we continued to fish as teenagers, we learned how to use artificial lures, which introduced us to another dimension of fishing.

Miss Margaret

CHAPTER 9

How to Tie a Proper Fishing Knot

ONE OF THE MOST important parts of fishing is learning how to properly tie a knot. Nothing is more frustrating than losing a fish because your knot came loose. A simple knot, such as the one used to tie your shoelaces, will not work. It isn't strong enough to stop a fish from pulling your knot apart. Anglers often use two very strong and easy to tie knots: the *Trilene knot* and the *Palomar knot*. With a little practice, you can learn to tie both! Be careful when you cinch or tighten your knots; hooks are sharp!

TRILENE KNOT

STEP 1: With your reel attached to the rod, and your line threaded through all of the eyes on your pole, pull off approximately 5 feet of line from the end of the rod. The hook will go on the end of the line. (The end of your fishing line is often referred to as the tag line.) Start by passing about 10 inches of line through the eye of the hook.

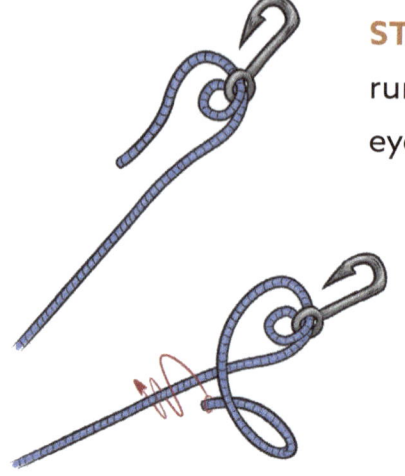

STEP 1B: Next, repeat the first step by running the end of the line through the eye of the hook in the same direction that you started, forming a half-inch loop.

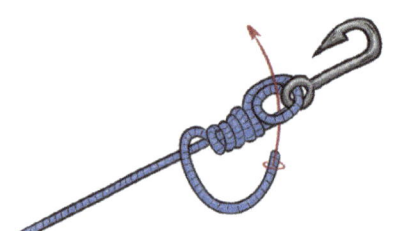

STEP 2: Wrap the tag line around the main line about six times.

STEP 3: Pass the end of the line through the double loop you formed in the first step.

STEP 4: Wet the knot with saliva from your mouth (very important). Wetting the knot prevents damage to the line and makes it easier to snug the knot tight. Pull the tag line (short piece of line) and the main line to form a knot. Using your thumb and index finger, hold the top of the knot and slide it down against the eye of the hook. Last, cut the tag line about a quarter of an inch above the eye of the hook.

PRO TIP:

The Palomar knot is the simplest of the two knots to tie.

PALOMAR KNOT

STEP 1: With your reel attached to the rod and your line threaded through all of the eyes on your pole, pull off approximately 5 feet of line from the end of the rod. Your hook ties onto the end of the line. To begin, thread about 15 inches of line through the eye of the hook. Next, take the end of the line and double back, threading the line back through the way you just came out. What you should wind up with is a 6 to 8 inch loop on one side of the eye of the hook and a double line with approximately 6 inches on the other side. See the picture to the left.

STEP 2: Take the end of the line with the loop and tie a loose-fitting overhand knot. The loop at the end of the overhand knot should be approximately 4 inches in length.

STEP 3: Pass the hook through the 4-inch loop. Next, holding the hook and the two lines above the overhand knot, pull the line so it begins to close around the eye of the hook. Before fully tightening the knot, wet the line with a little saliva from your mouth to prevent damaging the line, and then pull it tight. Finally, trim the extra line to about a quarter of an inch above the knot.

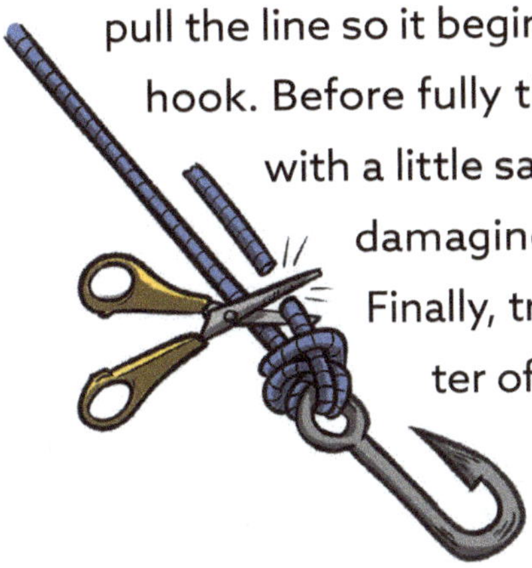

Patiently waiting for a bite.

Family, fishing, fun . . .

CHAPTER 10

How to Cast

LEARNING TO CAST IS an essential part of fishing. Spincast reels, baitcasters, and spinning reels (discussed earlier in the book) each release the line differently. With practice, you'll be able to accurately place your bait or lure exactly where you want it. Casting side arm, underhand, or overhand, all involve moving the rod behind you, quickly bringing it forward, and then releasing the line.

Spincast, baitcast, and spinning reels each cast differently as well, but the arm and wrist movement you use during casting is essentially the same no matter which reel you use.

To begin casting, hold the rod with your casting hand parallel to the ground at waist height. Your lure or bait should hang about 12 to 18 inches below the rod tip. Quickly raise your arm while bending your arm at the elbow, so the rod tip goes behind your head, and swiftly bring it forward pointing the rod tip toward your target. Release the line

A boy and his first largemouth bass

enabling the weight of your lure or bait to pull line off your reel. When reeling in your line and preparing for another cast, leave approximately 12 to 18 inches between the rod tip and your lure or bait. **Do not** reel your lure, bait, or bobber all the way in so it rests against the tip of your rod.

An easy way to gain experience with casting is to place a bucket or hula-hoop in your yard or other open space. Attach a half-ounce weight to the end of your line—you can substitute a metal washer or rubber stopper **(do not attach a hook or bobber)**—then practice casting into the bucket or hula-hoop. Keep in mind: When casting, do not look at your rod and reel; instead, look at the target you want to hit. As you gain more experience in the sport and begin to identify the fish habitats where you want to fish, being able to land your lure on the right spot is crucial.

PRO TIP:

Whether it's your first time going fishing, you've just bought a new reel, or you've only been fishing a couple of times, it's a good idea to practice casting before heading out. Having confidence in your ability to place your bait or lure exactly where you want it will help reduce the frustrations that come with being snagged or caught in trees, bushes, docks, and other entanglements. The ability to make an accurate cast will also help you catch more fish.

CASTING WITH A SPINCAST REEL

RELEASE BUTTON

Spincast reels are the easiest to use and are relatively inexpensive. They're a good option when fishing with live bait and excellent for beginners. Spincast reels are completely enclosed with a metal housing. The reel sits on top of the rod.

Follow the steps below to operate a spincast reel.

STEP 1: Push the button on the top of the reel down and hold it securely. This holds the line in place.

STEP 2: While keeping pressure on the button, bring the rod behind your head or to the side.

STEP 3: Quickly bring the rod forward. As it reaches the direction where you want your bait to land, release the button, which will release the line.

Keep in mind that before going fishing with a spincast reel, the drag must be properly set. More about drag is found earlier in the book.

CASTING WITH A SPINNING REEL

Spinning reels are preferred when casting lighter baits and lures. The reel is attached beneath the rod. Follow the steps below to cast.

STEP 1: Hold the reel with your casting hand. Use the tip of your index finger to hold the line. With your other hand, open the bail. The bail is the thick wire arm in front of the spool that flips up and down. When the bail is down (or closed), it stops line from coming off the reel. When the bail is down and the handle is turned, it takes up line. When the bail is open (flipped up), fishing line can come off the spool.

STEP 2: While holding the line with your index finger and the bail open with your other hand, bring the rod overhead and behind you or to the side.

STEP 3: Quickly bring the rod forward, aiming the tip of the rod toward your target and release the line with your finger, which will let the line go.

STEP 4: After the bait lands in the water, close the bail by hand or by turning the handle on the reel.

Remember that before going fishing with a spinning reel, the drag must be properly set. More about drag can be found earlier in this book.

CASTING WITH A BAITCAST REEL

Baitcast reels can be the most difficult to use, but they are worth learning how to operate. They are typically used with artificial lures. They work equally well when making an overhand or underhand cast. Before you head to the lake, adjust the reel to your liking and practice with it.

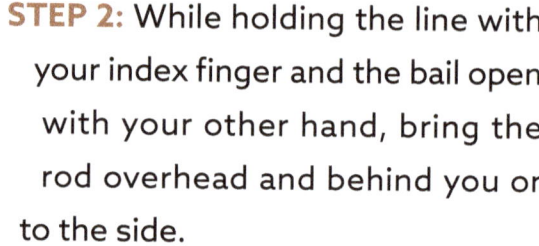

Baitcasters have four primary adjustments: the centrifugal brake, the magnetic brake, the spool tension adjustment, and the drag. Before fishing with a baitcaster, you should adjust each setting.

CENTRIFUGAL BRAKE: The centrifugal brake may be a one-time adjustment to your reel. It works during the first part of your cast helping to control the line as it comes off the spool with a lure attached. Before you attempt to adjust the brake, make a few practice casts to see if the factory setting is to your liking—it probably is, so you won't have to adjust this setting. You'll know if you have the ideal setting if the line comes off the spool at approximately the same speed that your lure travels. If your spool releases line faster than your lure travels, the line will backlash and tangle around the spool. If you do have to adjust the centrifugal brake, refer to your reel instruction manual. To adjust the centrifugal brake, you must remove the side panel of the reel. This is the primary reason that after setting it up once, you may not need to adjust it again.

MAGNETIC BRAKE: The magnetic brake is also used to control the rate/speed of the line as it comes off your spool during casting. This adjustment is found on the side of the reel. Adjusting the magnetic brake will slow or increase the rate of speed that the spool turns.

SPOOL TENSION: The spool tension knob applies tension to the spool. It's used to slow down and help stop the spool from spinning as the lure enters the water, preventing backlash. The adjustment knob is on the same side of the reel as the handle. Although it helps stop your lure at the end of your cast, it functions differently from magnetic and centrifugal brakes. This adjustment should never be used as an alternative to the brakes described above. Each time you put on a new lure you should check and set the spool tension. To check it, with your lure tied on, reel the lure close to the rod tip and push the release button. If the lure falls freely, the tension is too loose. Adjust it so the lure barely falls. If you press the release button and the lure does not fall, the tension is too tight. Adjust the setting so that when you release your lure and it hits the ground, the spool stops turning and does not create a backlash. Refer to the reel instruction manual for the location of this setting. Remember that you will need to set the spool tension adjustment with lures of different weights.

DRAG: As discussed earlier in the book, the drag is a safety mechanism. It allows your reel to release line if too much pull, or tension, is applied to your line after a fish bites. A properly set drag will be tight enough so that if a fish tries to dart away, some line will pull off the spool. As the fish tires and begins to stop fighting, the proper drag setting will allow you to take up line and reel the fish in.

THUMBING: In addition to the settings described above, on a baitcaster anglers use their thumb to slow the line as it comes off the spool. The way baitcasters operate makes using your thumb somewhat easy. Begin by holding the reel in your casting hand and placing your thumb on the spool to hold the line. While holding the spool/line, press the release button and make a cast by bringing the rod tip behind your head, or to the side, and then forward. As the rod reaches the direction where you want your lure to go, ease your thumb off the spool to let the line roll off. Many anglers maintain contact with the line as it comes off to reduce the chance of a backlash. If your lure begins to pull line off too quickly, applying pressure to the spool with your thumb can help stop line from coming off too fast.

Baitcasters are suitable for making overhand as well as underhand casts.

MAKING AN OVERHAND CAST

Follow the steps below to make an overhand cast:

STEP 1: Using your casting hand, place your thumb on the spool. Next, push and hold the release button making sure that your thumb holds the spool in place, so the line doesn't spool off.

STEP 2: Quickly bring the rod behind your head, or to the side, and quickly forward. As you bring the rod tip forward toward the target, ease your thumb off the spool to release the line while maintaining slight contact with the spool to prevent the line from coming off the reel too fast.

STEP 3: As your lure approaches the water, use your thumb to slow the line down, stopping it when it reaches the water.

MAKING AN UNDERHAND CAST

Another way to make a cast with a baitcaster is to make a *flip* or *pitch*. Both methods are performed by making an underhand motion with your rod. In this book, we'll talk about *pitching*. Most anglers pitch using lures, not live bait. It's an accurate method of casting a lure a short distance. Mastering the technique takes a bit of time and practice.

STEP 1: To begin, place the lure in one hand and take the rod in the other hand. Let out enough line so that with the rod tip at about 12 o'clock, the lure rests in your hand at about hip level.

STEP 2: Hold the lure between your index finger and thumb with the hook facing up and away from you, so when you're casting you don't stick yourself.

STEP 3: While eyeing your target and maintaining pressure on the spool, bring the rod tip down toward the target, and quickly lift it up, pulling the lure from between your fingers. As the lure moves forward in an underhand like motion, ease your thumb off the line releasing the lure while maintaining contact with the spool. The momentum of the lure will pull line off the spool as it moves toward the target. Use your thumb to slow your bait.

STEP 4: Once it hits the water, use your thumb to stop the spool and engage the reel.

UNDERHAND CASTING

CASTING TIPS

To avoid hitting someone, or getting your line tangled in a tree or bush, look behind you and to your left and right before casting.

When casting, point yourself toward the object you want to hit. Keep your eye on your target, not on your rod.

Whether you're fishing on the bottom or utilizing a bobber, let your bait sit in the water for a while after going into the water. After 30 seconds to a minute, with the rod tip in the air, lightly jerk the rod to move your bait. Then let it sit for another 30 seconds to a minute. If you do not get a bite after two minutes, reel the line in and cast again. Be patient. Anglers often make several casts to the same location to trigger a bite.

Whether fishing on the bottom or with a bobber, try to keep slack out of your line. To accomplish this, simply reel up the extra line.

If you think you have a bite because your line or bobber moves, you feel a tug, or your bobber is pulled under water, you should set the hook. Setting the hook is done by quickly pointing your rod tip down toward your bait and taking up any slack in the line. Then with one sharp jerk, pull the rod tip up to the 11 o'clock position. The motion of pulling your rod tip up quickly will force the hook into the fish's mouth.

Be vigilant. Watch your line, rod tip, and bobber for any unusual movement. Try to keep your line tight and the rod tip up.

One last tip. Never go into the water to retrieve your pole or a fishing lure. Occasionally, a fishing pole slips out of your hand, or a lure breaks off and drops into the water. Do not go in the water after a lure or rod. Chalk it up to experience.

PRO TIP:

If your lure goes straight into the air instead of forward when you cast, you may have released the line too soon. Wait a bit longer to release the line next time. If your bait slams hard into the water a few feet in front of you, chances are you released the line too late. Try releasing it sooner on your next cast.

Three amigos enjoying time together.

CHAPTER 11

Using Artificial Lures

INSTEAD OF USING LIVE bait, anglers often fish with artificial lures. They are designed to look like, or mimic, items that fish normally eat, like frogs, crawfish, minnows, and other aquatic life, and trigger them to feed. Although, many families of lures don't look like real-life creatures at all. At times, lures can be more effective at enticing fish to bite than live bait. Artificial lures require anglers to manipulate them in the water by bouncing them on the bottom, retrieving them, jerking them through the water, or sometimes pulling them and letting them rest.

Artificial lures come in thousands of styles, colors, sizes, and functions. Below are a few of the most common families of lures. This is by no means a complete list. As you gain experience fishing, experiment with different styles, weights, sizes, techniques, and applications. By doing so, you will become a more skillful angler.

PRO TIP:

Experiment with different ways of retrieving your artificial lure, like stopping and starting, bouncing it on the bottom, twitching it on top of the water, or dragging it on the bottom.

SOFT PLASTIC LURES

Soft plastics are one of the most popular types of artificial lures. They come in a variety of colors, shapes, sizes, and applications. These lures are designed to resemble and mimic creatures such as worms, frogs, crawfish, and minnows. Soft plastics can be rigged a number of ways to run along the bottom, middle of the water column, or on top.

Most soft plastic lures come without hooks or weights. This provides the angler with the option to fish them with some weight or none at all. This means you can fish soft plastics near the surface, middle, and bottom of the lake. It is a very popular and very effective style of bait.

CRANK BAITS

Crank baits are a class of lures designed to mimic small baitfish, like bluegills, shad, or perch as they move through the water. They can also resemble small crustaceans, like crawfish or insects. Most crank baits have a small plastic bill or lip in front that causes the lure to dive into the water and run at a specific depth and "wobble" slightly back and forth giving the lure a unique action as it's pulled through the water. Generally, the larger the bill, the deeper a crankbait will dive and run.

They're very easy to use because they only require the angler to cast it out and reel it in.

SPINNER BAITS

Spinner baits are artificial baits made of stiff wire that is shaped somewhat like a *V*. At one end is a weighted hook and at the other end is one, two, or three blades that spin when the lure is retrieved. These lures mimic the motion of a small fish swimming through the water. Spinner baits are very easy to use only requiring the angler to cast them and reel them in, just like crank baits.

TOP WATER LURES

Most *top water lures* are designed to float on the surface of the water. Some sink to a certain depth. Others are designed to suspend in the water. Top water baits require the angler to work the bait. To do this, hold the rod tip downward toward the water and then snap the rod tip toward you, causing the lure to jerk forward in the water. Then rest the lure and repeat the process. Often fish will strike the lure as it rests in the water.

JIGS

Jigs are lures that have a lead or tungsten weight head that's round, football shaped, or oblong that has a hook molded into it with an eye for tying your line on. Most jigs come with a rubber or silicon *skirt*, or feathers attached to them that add motion to the jig when it's in the water. Others come with no skirts and are simply a hook and weight.

Most jigs are used to fish along the bottom with some sort of plastic lure attached to the hook that adds additional motion and bulk, making the jig look like a crawfish. The jig can also be retrieved by swimming it through the water, bouncing it on the bottom, or dragging it.

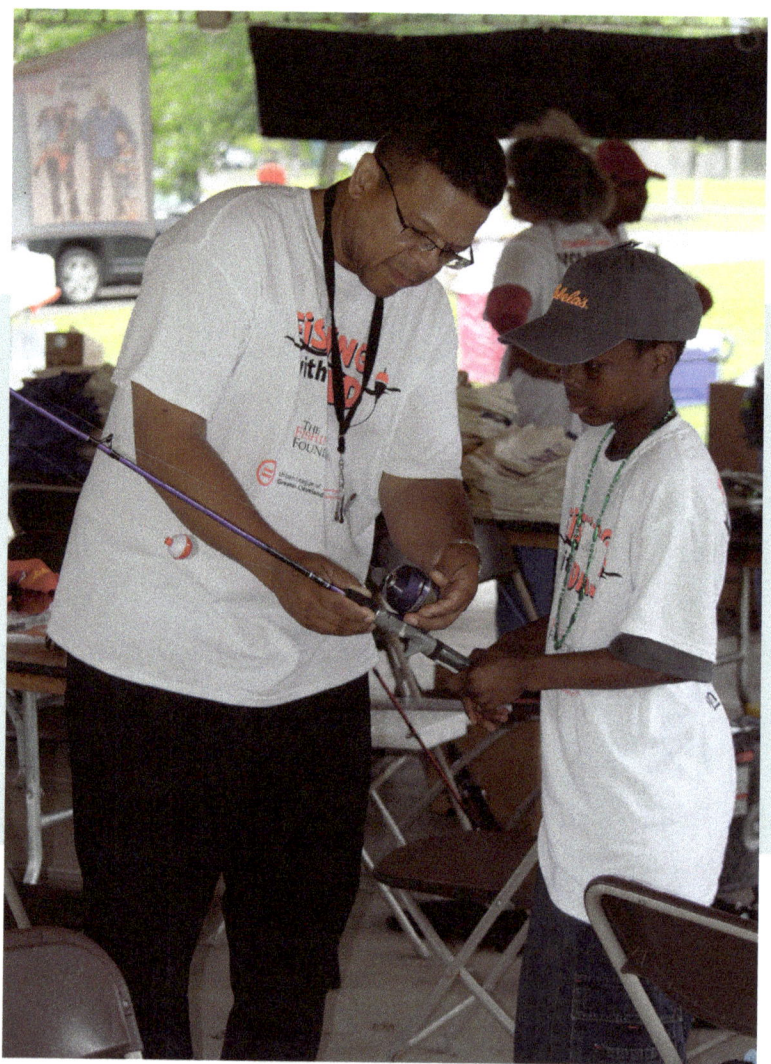

Showing a young participant how it all works.

CHAPTER 12

Fish Habitat and Handling

FISH CAN BE FOUND in most bodies of water such as ponds, rivers, and lakes. Even if you live in the city, you can probably find a good place to fish. In most states, you'll find a department of natural resources that oversees state-owned bodies of water. Such organizations stock rivers, lakes, and ponds and often establish places for anglers to fish. In some cases, municipal governments or local park organizations provide similar services and can help you find places to fish. Other great resources include local bait shops, friends, and neighbors. If you have access to a computer, many organizations help anglers find places to fish by simply putting in your zip code and searching. Once you do find a place to fish, make sure that it's either a public waterway, or if it is privately owned, that you have permission to fish there.

When deciding on a place to fish, look for bodies of water that are clean and appear healthy. One indication of the health of the lake is the health of the shoreline and the body of water itself. Is it clear of debris? Is there an abundance of grass, trees, shrubs, and wildlife in the area? The condition of the surrounding land is a good indication that the body of water is clean and has plenty of food and vegetation. Together these things make a great fish habitat. A clean and healthy environment provides fish a place to feed, rest, reproduce, and flourish.

An abundance of vegetation is a key component to a healthy environment. Vegetation provides a place for zooplankton (small organisms), small insects, and small fish to hide and grow, thereby becoming a food source for bigger fish. In addition, vegetation releases oxygen into the water.

For fish to have a healthy habitat, people must take good care of lakes and streams so fish and other wildlife can survive. To maintain a healthy habitat, do not pollute the water by pouring harmful liquids or solids in the water or throwing your trash in the water.

SETTING THE HOOK

After a fish takes your bait or lure, you need to bring it in, or land it. Landing a fish begins with firmly planting the hook in the fish's mouth. This process is commonly referred to as **setting the hook.** When a fish strikes, quickly lower your rod tip down toward the water and quickly reel in the slack. Then rapidly and forcibly, lift the rod tip up to cause the hook to penetrate the mouth of the fish. Generally, the motion made to set the hook uses your wrist, arm, and elbow.

If you see your line or bobber move or feel a slight tug on the line, then it's time to set the hook. There are times when a fish takes your bait, or lure, and you do not feel it move. If you watch your rod tip, or where your line enters the water, you may see your line move. If this happens, set the hook.

There are times for being a bit patient before setting the hook. Often, fish peck at your bait before taking it. If you set the hook

before the fish has your bait or lure, you'll pull the hook out of its mouth and miss the bite.

Setting the hook is a bit of a balancing act. If you do not forcefully set the hook to penetrate the fish's mouth, you will lose the fish. If you set the hook too hard, you run the risk of tearing the hook through the fish's mouth or breaking your line. Be patient. The more fish you catch the better an angler you become.

CONTROLLING THE FISH

After successfully hooking a fish, you must control it so you can bring it to shore or into the boat. This process is often referred to as playing the fish, which helps tire the fish so it's easier to bring in.

To control the fish after setting the hook, it is important to keep the rod tip in the air. By keeping the rod tip up, the bend in the rod will maintain pressure on the fish, tire it out, and keep the hook in its mouth. If your drag is properly set, you can reel the fish in and still allow the fish to pull more line if it surges. This will help you to avoid breaking the line while the fish tires out, so you can finish reeling it in.

Beginning anglers are often tempted to jerk and reel a fish in by cranking the reel as quickly as possible. By doing this, you run the risk of losing the fish.

PRO TIP:

Keep the fish away from objects in the water like weeds, rocks, poles, bushes, or trees. If your line gets tangled around an object, you may lose your fish. To steer the fish, try moving your rod left or right, keeping your rod tip up. This will maintain pressure on your fish. If your fish does get tangled around an object, continue to maintain pressure on the fish. Many times, the fish will work itself lose and you can reel it in.

If the fish surges forward, reel in the slack.

If the fish swims away, stop reeling in and allow the drag to release a bit of line. As soon as the fish stops pulling out line, reel in the slack.

When the fish tires and stops pulling out line, it's ok to pump and reel the fish in. To do so, lift the rod tip, this pulls the fish toward you. While maintaining pressure on the fish, lower the rod tip and take up the slack in the line. Repeat this process until the fish is close enough to land it by hand or with a net.

LANDING THE FISH

The phrase "landing the fish" refers to getting it out of the water. The easiest way to land a fish is with a net. Using a net is no guarantee of securing it. Here are a few things to keep in mind: Bring the fish in close enough so the net can easily reach the fish. Ease the net into the water away from the fish as not to alarm it. If you spook the fish, it may turn away and make another run, and you may end up losing it.

The one that didn't get away.

When netting a fish, do not chase it. With the net in the water, guide the fish into the net, or slowly move the net under the fish and swoop the net upwards, landing the fish. Quickly remove the net and fish from the water.

If you do not have a net and the fish is not too heavy, you can often lift the fish out of the water or drag it to shore. If you are careful and are not catching fish with sharp teeth, you can carefully bring the fish close to you and insert your thumb in its mouth. Then, with your index finger, grab the fish's lower jaw and lift it out the water. Do not enter the water to land your fish.

PRO TIP:

Remember to properly set the drag before you fish. Keep your rod tip up and your line tight.

Learning the ropes.

CHAPTER 13

What to Do After You Catch a Fish

A GROWING NUMBER OF anglers fish just for fun, to be with friends, and to enjoy nature. For these anglers, catching fish is only part of the experience, so once they've reeled it in, they let it go. This practice is known as catch and release. At The Fishing Foundation we encourage anglers to catch and release. Fish that are caught and quickly released survive the experience.

Here are some guidelines on how to handle a fish you plan to release:

- When handling a fish, treat it gently and be careful when you remove the hook.
- Take care not to drop the fish on the ground.
- Be very careful not to stick yourself on the fins of the fish.
- Fish have a natural slime on their body. Do not remove it. It protects their skin.
- Fish use gills on the side of their body to breathe. Do not injure them.
- Return the fish to the water as soon as possible.
- Some fish have teeth. Be careful not to cut yourself.
- Catfish have whiskers. They don't sting; it's a misconception. The whiskers are used to detect food.
- Do not harm a fish's eyes.

If you do decide to harvest, or keep your fish to eat, you can put them on a stringer, such as a piece of rope or a commercial stringer made of metal, and then place the fish in the water. Be sure to tie the stringer securely on shore. This should keep the fish alive until you've finished fishing and will prevent them from swimming away. The other, more preferred method is to place the fish in a cooler on ice.

TIPS ON FISHING FROM SHORE

Fishing requires patience. When casting, lines get tangled, hooks get caught in bushes, grass, and trees. There will be times when you lose your equipment, and you'll need to retie. So, always carry extra fishing gear with you in your tackle box.

The best way to detect a bite is to hold the rod steady. If you're fishing on the bottom, keep tension on your line to detect movement in the line indicating that you might have a fish. If you're using a bobber, keep your eyes on it. If it begins to move or bob up and down, you might have a fish. Whichever method you use, stay vigilant for any movement of your line or rod.

Target structures in the water. Fish like to hang around objects in the water that make them feel safe and provide shade or a place to ambush other fish. Brush piles, sunken trees, branches, and man-made structures placed in the water are great places to fish.

On days with a slight breeze, the wind can push bait and other food in the direction the wind is blowing. These areas often attract the larger fish you are looking for.

If you're a beginning angler, practice casting before you go fishing. Set up a target in the yard and see how close you can come to it.

Be a good steward of the environment. Do not leave behind trash or pollute the water. Take everything with you when you leave, including gum wrappers, plastic containers, cans, and used fishing gear. Keeping our waters and land clean is the single most important thing you can do when fishing.

Learn to tie a strong knot. If your knot comes loose with a fish on the line, you will be upset.

Slow down. After making a great cast do not be in a hurry to bring your line in. Take the time to fish a great looking area before moving to another spot. After thoroughly working an area with no bites, try another bait or move a bit to another location. When you do find the fish, work the area. After the fishing slows down, give the spot a rest. Leave and fish another spot and return in an hour or so to see if more fish have returned.

Anticipate getting a bite. When it happens, stay calm, set the hook, and keep your rod tip up. When you're reeling in, maintain pressure on the line. Often, beginning anglers become distracted, do not think about the bite, and miss fish because they simply are not paying attention when a fish bites.

When you're searching for fish, do it as quietly as possible. Fish can hear extremely well. Unusual noise and sudden movements can chase them away. Fish can detect movement even when you're fishing from shore or from a boat.

Lending a helping hand.

Landing his first largemouth bass.

A small fish, a big accomplishment, landing her first fish.

CHAPTER 14

Recommended Equipment for Beginning Anglers

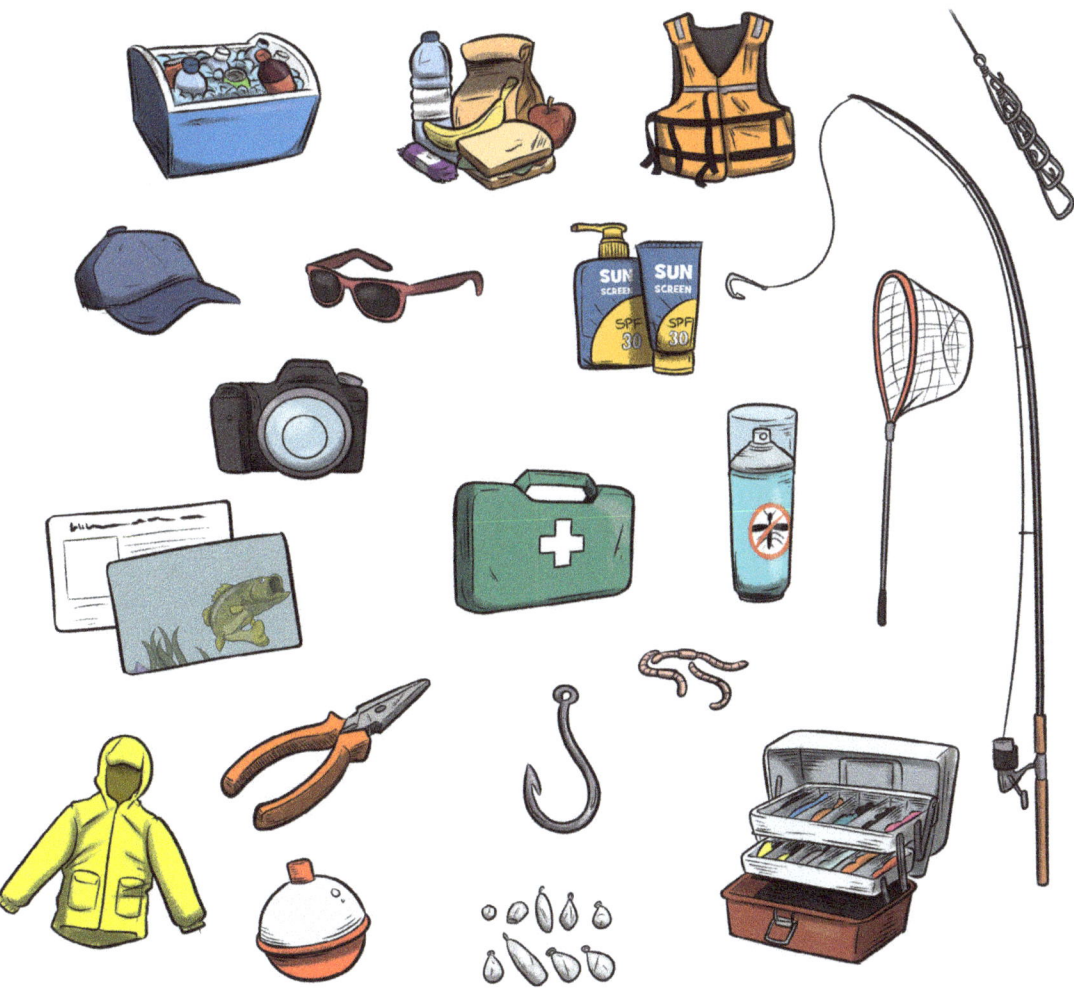

Use the list below as a starting checklist as you prepare to go fishing. Consider bringing extras of the tackle you might lose, such as hooks, bobbers, and weights.

- A **5- to 6-foot medium action rod and spincasting reel** is a great rod and reel for beginners because it's easy to operate and is inexpensive.

- **Eight-pound monofilament line**, also known as mono, is a good choice because it's very durable and inexpensive.

- A **#6 hook** is a great choice for beginning anglers. These hooks work for pan fish as well as larger fish like bass and catfish.

- A pair of **needle-nose pliers** is an important tool for removing hooks from your fish.

- **Quarter-ounce weights** such as split-shots are easy to attach and remove because they squeeze to the line with a pair of pliers.

- A round, 1.5-inch **plastic bobber** is a great starting point. It is easy to attach and will provide enough buoyancy to fish on the surface of the water.

- A **large bucket** is always good to have around. You can place gear, bait, and other items in it; you can sit on it; and you can even keep your fish in it.

- You'll need plenty of **bait** such as earthworms, minnows, maggots, or wax worms.

- It's a good idea to pack **a rag or paper towels** for cleaning your hands. Remember, do not litter.

- Don't forget your **camera**! You'll want to capture all the fun moments.

- Check with your state wildlife officials to see if a **fishing license** is required.

- Don't forget your **hat, sunglasses, and sunscreen**. One sure way to ruin your good time is to come home with a sunburn.
- Find a **clean body of water** to fish.
- You're going to get hungry so make sure to bring **refreshments and lunch**.
- Pack rain gear.
- Use a tackle box to hold your gear.
- This is one you definitely don't want to forget: **lots of patience**.

GLOSSARY

action: Action refers to where the rod bends when weight is applied to it. Rod action may be slow, medium, fast, or anything in between (e.g., medium-fast). The action will influence how far an angler can cast, the responsiveness when a fish takes a hook, and the action felt when reeling the fish in.

aught: Term used to describe the measurement of a hook. Aught-sized hooks are identified by a forward slash (/). They are written as 3/0 and pronounced three aught. They start at size 1/0 and go up one number at a time (1/0, 2/0, 3/0, and so forth). A 6/0 aught hook is larger than a 1/0 aught hook.

backlash: When the line on the spool of a reel becomes tangled. This often occurs when casting into the wind, the line is loose around the spool, or the line comes off the reel too quickly.

baitcast reel: Also known as a baitcaster, this type of reel allows you to cast lures like jigs, spinner baits, and crankbaits with pinpoint accuracy. The line is spooled onto a drum and there is a dialed-in drag resistance. Baitcast reels require a higher skill set to be able to thumb the spool as line flows off.

bobber: A flotation device that attaches to a fishing line and suspends a bait at a predetermined depth.

braid fishing line: Any fishing line, woven from strands of cloth or fibrous material. Braid lines are extremely durable and sensitive.

crank bait: A family of bait made from hardwood or plastic material with a plastic lip that causes the bait to dive under water mimicking the motion of a fish or other creature.

eyes: Also known as guides, they serve to direct your line along the rod to your target. Guides also contribute to a rod's sensitivity and casting distance.

fluorocarbon line: A fishing line made from a specialty plastic, called fluoropolymer (PVDF) material. Also known as fluoro, it has very little stretch and is nearly invisible in the water.

jig: A lure that consists of a lead sinker with a hook molded into it. Often jigs are covered by a skirt made out of strands of rubber or silicone that ungulate in the water to attract fish. Typically, jigs are fished on the bottom by dragging or hopping them.

monofilament line: Also known as mono, this fishing line is made from a single fiber of plastic-like material known as polymers. Mono is buoyant and is effective when used with lures that float.

olfactory bulb: This allows organisms to interact with their environment by the detection of odor signals.

otoliths: Commonly known as earstones, otoliths are hard, calcium carbonate structures located directly behind the brain of bony fish.

Palomar knot: A Palomar knot, used for securing fishing line to fishing hooks, is a steady and reliable knotting technique. Palomar knots can also be used on both braided fishing line and thin, monofilament fishing line, which makes them versatile. When done correctly, this easy to tie knot is considered one of the most dependable variations of fishing knots.

Power: This describes a rod's strength and resistance to bending.

PFD: A personal flotation device, or PFD, is a life jacket, life preserver, or life vest. A life jacket is designed to hold your head above water so you can breathe. No matter which type of PFD is available, it won't work if you don't wear it!

setting the hook: The act of planting the hook into the mouth of a biting fish.

shad: This fish species has a dark blue colored back; the rest of its body is light silver; and its underbelly is white. You can distinguish this species by the short row of dark colored spots along its shoulder. Most adults measure about 22 inches long and weigh about 5 pounds or so. However, they can range in size between 17 and 30 inches in length.

skirt: Strands of rubber or silicone that attach to a lure such as jig or spinner bait.

soft plastics: Soft plastic lures, commonly called soft plastics, are a family of artificial bait used to fish on the surface, middle of the water column, and bottom. The advantage of using soft plastic over hard bodied lures is that when a fish strikes a soft plastic bait, it feels natural so the fish will hold the lure longer in its mouth, giving the angler extra time to set the hook. Most soft plastic lures are produced by heating plastic into a liquid form then pouring it into a mold to replicate the shape of a grub, worm, baitfish, crawfish, lizard, frog, or insect.

spincast reel: A type of reel fitted with a plastic cover. On the rear of the reel there's a button that when pushed holds the line and when let go releases the line. The line emerges from a small hole at the front of the reel. Because the line is covered by a plastic housing, spincast reels do not become tangled as easily as spinning reels do.

spinner bait: A lure in the shape of a *V* or *L* with a weighted head and rubber skirt and hook on one arm and spinner blades on the other arm.

spinning reel: A spinning reel is designed to attach beneath the rod. The line wraps around the spool, and a metal arm called the bail keeps the line in place. When the bail is opened, it releases the line.

strike: When a fish bites, it is known as a strike.

top water lure: A family of bait that floats on top of the water. Anglers use the motion of the rod to move these lures in an erratic motion across the top of the water.

Trilene knot: A multi-purpose fishing knot that can be used to attach monofilament line to hooks, swivels, and lures.

weight: Also known as a sinker, a weight is a small piece of round, bullet, or teardrop shaped metal that clips, threads, or ties onto a fishing line to sink a bait or lure to the bottom.

zooplankton: Small floating or weakly swimming organisms that drift with water currents and are part of the food chain.

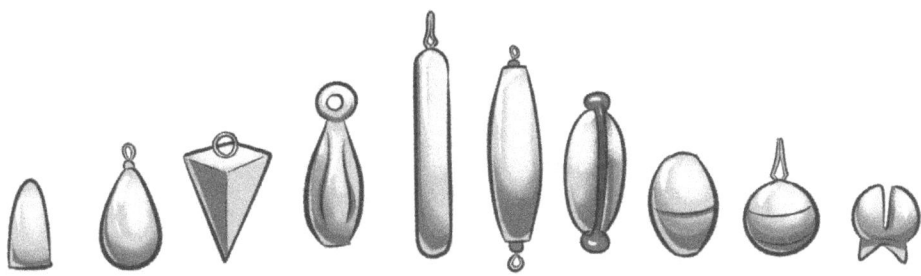

Dennis and Gail

About the Authors

GAIL ANN GRIZZELL

Gail Ann Grizzell has always had a desire to help people. When Gail was a youngster in Berea, Ohio, she began volunteering as a candy striper at the local hospital. She continued her volunteer endeavors assisting youth organizations, which ultimately led to a 35-year career in the field of philanthropy as a nonprofit and marketing fundraising professional, with the United Negro College Fund and Ideastream, the public broadcasting affiliate radio and television stations in Cleveland, Ohio. Gail decided to combine her fundraising skills with her passion for fishing—a passion inspired by her mother, Margaret—and in partnership with Dennis James Knowles co-founded The Fishing Foundation. Now retired, Gail devotes her time, treasure, talent, and touch to expanding the programming of the Foundation. In addition to spending time with her family, Gail serves in a leadership role with The Fishing Foundation, enjoys international and national travel, reading, cooking, gardening, attending arts and cultural events, and most of all, fishing. Along with her sister and business partner, Gail also co-owns Executive Meeting Planners, LLC, a minority- and women-owned-and-operated meeting planning small business enterprise. Gail holds a Bachelor of Arts degree from The Ohio State University.

DENNIS JAMES KNOWLES

Growing up in Shaker Heights, Ohio, Dennis James Knowles was never into organized sports. He did participate in neighborhood pick-up games like basketball, touch football, and kickball, but he never had the calling to pursue sports—until he was introduced to fishing. Dennis first picked up a rod and reel when he was 12 years old on a summer vacation to Milwaukee, Wisconsin. His uncle Ulysses Tidwell was an avid angler, and Dennis was eager to learn. For many years to follow, Dennis returned to Milwaukee for two weeks of camping, fishing, fun, and adventure.

When he went on to college at Ohio University, Dennis took along his rods and reels and went fishing on the weekends. After earning an undergraduate degree in journalism and completing his Master of Fine Arts in film production, Dennis returned to his hometown of Cleveland, Ohio, and entered the field of television. Eventually, he became a member of a local fishing club, North Coast Bass Anglers Association, serving as its president and tournament director for several years. It was during this time that he and Gail A. Grizzell founded The Fishing Foundation, a non-profit organization dedicated to improving people's lives through fishing.

THE FISHING FOUNDATION

The Fishing Foundation (TFF) is a 501(c)(3) non-profit organization; its mission is to enrich people's lives through the sport of fishing. The Fishing Foundation programming includes classroom instruction in four specific areas: aquatic education, casting, water safety, and identifying local fish species, as well as training in how to fish from shore in a safe and secure environment.

Launched in 2012, The Fishing Foundation has touched the lives of hundreds of children, teens, and adults. Most importantly, The Fishing Foundation provides youngsters residing in underserved areas a unique opportunity to connect with others, commune with nature, and expand their environmental experience.

To learn more about The Fishing Foundation, please visit:
www.thefishingfoundation.org.

If you've enjoyed *Learn to Fish: A Step-by-Step Guide for Beginning Anglers*, we would be grateful for a review on Amazon, Goodreads or any place where the book is sold.